THE STRENGTH
OF A SURVIVOR

Mae Carol Clark Jackson Waldon

DEDICATION

To every reader walking through storms you never asked for may this book remind you that God sees you, God hears you, and God will carry you.

I give this testimony so you know you are never alone.

Hold on to your faith, even when the path is dark.

What He did for me, He can do for you. **Amen**

TABLE OF CONTENTS

ABOUT THE AUTHOR

My name is Mae Carol Walter, and my life is a testimony of strength, endurance, and unshakable faith. I was born and raised in Texas, and throughout my years, I have walked through trials that could have broken me, but by God's grace, I kept rising with courage and a heart anchored in Him. My story is one of overcoming hardship, surviving loss, and holding on to hope even in the darkest seasons.

I have always dedicated myself to serving others in every way I could. I worked as a nurse assistant for more than thirty years, caring for patients with compassion and dignity. I also served as a cashier for the state of Texas, bringing professionalism, kindness, and integrity to my daily interactions. My commitment to honest work and helping people has always extended beyond my jobs, I have been a commissioned notary for the State of Texas since the 1970s, faithfully serving my community for decades.

I am also a proud member of the Order of the Eastern Star, a position I have held since 1973. My involvement reflects my values of service, fellowship, and spiritual integrity principles that have guided and grounded me throughout my life.

Despite everything I have endured betrayal, sickness, heartbreak, and the loss of loved ones, I continued to stand tall and keep my mind focused on the responsibilities before me. I often say that even in the midst of trouble, God gave me the strength to hold down a job, care for my family, and walk with dignity.

Today, I share my testimony so others may find hope in their own journeys. My story is a reminder that no matter what comes, faith can lift you, truth can free you, and God can carry you through anything. This book is my gift to every reader who needs encouragement, healing, or the assurance that miracles still happen.

INTRODUCTION

A LIFE OF STRUGGLE AND SURVIVAL

My name is Mae Carol Clark Jackson Waldon, and my story is not an easy one to tell. From my earliest years, my life has been marked by struggle some of it physical, some of it emotional, and much of it far heavier than a child should ever have to carry. Yet even through those dark times, I found a way to keep going. What I share in these pages is not just a list of hardships, but a testimony of how faith and determination can carry a person forward when everything else seems to be falling apart.

As a little girl, I faced things that should have broken me mistreatment, exploitation, and pain that I often kept hidden. Later, as a woman, I walked through trials that tested my spirit again and again: losing people I loved, surviving violence, and trying to stand tall in a world that was not always kind. Each battle left a scar, but each scar also became a reminder that I was still standing.

This book is about more than survival; it is about learning how to live again after being hurt. It is about choosing forgiveness over bitterness, faith over fear, and hope over despair. My belief in God gave me strength when I had none of my own, and my trust in His plan helped me rise when life tried to keep me down.

I know there are many who have walked through struggles like mine. For you, I want this story to be more than a witness of pain I want it to be a reminder that healing is possible, and that no matter how deep the wound, you can still rise again. My journey is not perfect, but it is real. And it begins here, with the story of a woman who refused to give up.

CHAPTER 1

EARLY YEARS AND FAMILY STRUGGLES

My initial years were troubled with the massive emotional turmoil & hard experiences, many of which altered me into the strongest woman I am now. My childhood revolved around the severe challenges within my family, where love & assistance were rare. The most disturbing experience came when I was 15 years old & my father attempted intimacy with me, and when I would tell my mom, she would reply to go away, accusing me of lying. This specific moment of betrayal used to get me disturbed for years & deepen the ongoing emotional scars.

The particular emotional ignorance & verbal exploitation I suffered from my parents made me feel worthless & unloved. My father's extremely cruel words, "You ain't going to be nothing," stayed in my mind, contributed to damage my confidence & eliminate my hope. With my dreams repeatedly crushed & suppressed, I discovered myself getting trapped in a highly suffocating environment. My hopes of tap dancing, interior decorator & even becoming a court reporter or a successful legislator were diminished before they could even start.

Despite the continual rejection, I discovered ways to run away. I sought comfort in tiny moments of freedom through daydreaming about a pain-free life. But the intense pain caused by my father's actions, along with the emotional toll of growing up in such a challenging environment, left super deep emotional wounds that took years to heal for me. My sense of self was damaged & the emotional negligence I dealt with amid these decisive years shaped the way I pictured myself & my relationships with others.

Even as I battled with abuse & emotional ignorance, I did not lose hope & moved forward. My strength and my survival ability made me escape through the night of my initial life. The childhood hardships of mine strengthened my resilience & ability to stay firm amid dozens of wrongdoings.

This chapter will have made you explore clearly how my initial life experiences affected me & despite it all, I knew my path to survive. The abuse & emotional hardship I witnessed during these years changed my life, but they also ensured me the strength to tackle the challenges that are ahead.

CHAPTER 2

FALLING IN LOVE AND FINDING HOPE

After all those years of being told I wasn't nothing, that I'd never be nothing, I just needed to get away. At fifteen years old, with daddy's betrayal still fresh and mama refusing to believe me, I felt trapped in that house. Every dream I ever had, tap dancing, interior decorator, becoming a court reporter, or even a legislator, they shot them all down. "You ain't going to be shit," they'd say. "Get on somewhere." Those words fractured my ego something terrible, made me feel smaller than I already was.

One day, I walked to the store, just trying to get some air, trying to breathe outside those suffocating walls. That's when I stumbled upon Dave Jackson. Lord, he was something handsome, well-dressed, driving a nice car. He looked like hope itself rolling down that street. We started seeing each other secretly. He was older than me, I believe about five years, but I didn't care about that. After what happened with daddy, I was just ready to get out of that house. Ready to start living a life that felt like my own.

It wasn't long before I got pregnant with my first son. My daddy nicknamed him Post Toasties because that boy loved cereal more than anything in this world. He'd eat Post Toasties morning, noon, and night if I let him. Dave wanted to marry me right away, but his mama wouldn't have it. She thought I wasn't good enough for her son. He was her only child, and she had other plans for him, plans that didn't include a young girl like me.

But my mama wasn't going for that. She told them straight up that if Dave didn't marry me, she'd file statutory rape charges. So the judge married us, and for a little while, I thought maybe this was it. Maybe this was my chance at something better.

Shortly after we got married, Dave was drafted into the army. Two years, they said. While he was gone, my son and I received alottment every month. I was young, but I was managing. I was being a mother, taking care of my baby, and dreaming about the life we'd have when Dave came home.

When he finally came home, we moved together to a little town called Manor, Texas. It was quiet there, peaceful in a way I'd never known growing up. For the first time in my life, I felt like maybe I could have something normal. Something good.

Christmas morning came, and I remember it so clearly. Dave got up early and prepared our dinner. He got our son dressed up nice, and they went visiting. He took Postosis to mama's house so she could babysit while Dave and I planned to go out on the town that evening. It was supposed to be our special night together, celebrating the holiday, celebrating being a family.

But it didn't happen like that.

Dave went to a pool hall that afternoon. Got into an argument with some guy. And just like that, he was shot dead. My husband. The father of my child. Gone on Christmas Day.

I was so hurt I could barely stand. I didn't even weigh about 125 pounds, and I didn't know it at the time, but I was pregnant. When they told me Dave was gone, when I stood at that grave watching them lower my husband into the ground, I lost our baby right there. The grief was so heavy it took the life growing inside me.

For five years after that, I grieved. I didn't have an affair with anyone. Didn't even look at another man. I was just trying to survive, trying to raise my son by myself, trying to understand why God would give me a taste of hope just to snatch it away so violently. I was a widow before I even really got to be a wife. A single mother, before I'd barely learned what it meant to be married.

Those were dark years. Heavy years. But somehow, with God's help, I kept going. I had to. My son needed me, and I wasn't going to let him down the way I'd been let down. I wasn't going to give up, even when giving up seemed like the easiest thing in the world.

CHAPTER 3

LOSS, GRIEF, AND RESILIENCE

After five years of grieving Dave, I finally got myself together. The wound was still there, but I'd learned how to live with it. That's when I met Johnny Williams from Oklahoma. We started dating, and things seemed good at first. He treated me nice, made me laugh, and I thought maybe God was giving me another chance at happiness.

We got married, and I had a seven-pound, eight-ounce baby boy. We named him Johnny Jr., but we called him "Mister" because he was so smart, even as a little thing. He was the cutest little rascal, bald-headed and bright-eyed. With my two boys, Postosis and little Mister, I thought we were building something. A real family.

Big Johnny loved to gamble, and he drank. Now, that was all right with me as long as he took care of home. As long as the bills got paid, the boys had what they needed, and we had food on the table, I could live with his habits. But when that stopped, when he started spending the money we needed on his gambling and drinking, I knew I had to do something.

I asked for a divorce. He wasn't having that. He got angry, real angry, but I stood my ground. I filed for divorce anyway and moved from where we lived to another apartment. I thought putting some distance between us would help, would give us both time to cool down and figure things out.

The boys and I spent time together at mama's house one evening. We had a good time, just being together, being safe. When we got home that night, I started preparing my boys' bath. They were tired and ready to get cleaned up and go to bed.

Then Big Johnny busted in through the back door.

I didn't even have time to react. He came at me with a knife and stabbed me twenty-seven times. Twenty-seven times. I only weighed about 125 pounds. There wasn't much of me to begin with, and he was trying to make sure there was nothing left.

My two boys were screaming and hollering, scared out of their minds. My oldest, Postosis, he ran next door and asked the people to call the police. That boy saved my life. If he hadn't done that, if he'd frozen up or been too scared to move, I wouldn't be here telling this story.

That's all I remember from that night. Everything after that is just blank.

I woke up in the hospital. They told me I'd been there about two weeks. I'd lost so much blood that it was a miracle I lived. A miracle. The doctors couldn't explain it with my size and that many stab wounds, I should have died right there in that apartment. But God wasn't done with me yet.

When I got out of the hospital, I stayed at mama's. I couldn't go back to that apartment. Couldn't even think about it. I learned there was a house in the neighborhood for sale, so I looked into it and purchased it. I needed somewhere safe for my boys, somewhere Big Johnny couldn't find us.

But when they released me from the hospital, I couldn't walk. The wounds had done something to my body, left me weak and unable to stand on my own. My brothers took turns packing me wherever I needed to go. They'd lift me up, carry me from room to room, take me to appointments. I was dependent on everybody, and that was hard for a woman who'd always tried to stand on her own two feet.

But by the help of the Lord, I overcame that situation. Slowly, bit by bit, I began to heal. My body got stronger. I learned to walk again, learned to do things for myself. I began to live a normal life, or as normal as life can be after something like that.

I became the mother and the father for my two boys. I had to be both. They'd seen too much already: their mama getting stabbed, the blood, the screaming, the chaos. I had to show them that we could survive this. That we could be all right.

Looking back now, I believe I was a little too strict on them. I was so scared of losing them, so scared of them going down the wrong path, that I held on too tight. I wanted to protect them from everything, but you can't always do that. Sometimes you have to let them learn, let them make mistakes, even when it breaks your heart to watch.

But in those early days after the stabbing, all I knew was that God had spared my life for a reason. He'd let me live when I should have died. And I wasn't going to waste that gift. I was going to raise my boys right, give them a better life than I had, and show them that no matter how many times life knocks you down, you can get back up.

That's what resilience is. It's not about never getting hurt. It's about getting hurt and choosing to keep going anyway. It's about looking death in the face and saying, "Not today." It's about believing that God has a purpose for your pain, even when you can't see it yet.

I was hurt. I was scared. But I was alive. And as long as I had breath in my body, I was going to use it to love my boys and praise the God who saved me.

CHAPTER 4

DOMESTIC VIOLENCE AND ITS AFTERMATH

The stabbing wasn't the first time Johnny hurt me. It was just the worst time. The time that almost ended everything.

When I say I went through a lot of domestic violence, I mean I lived in it. It wasn't just that one night when he came through that back door with a knife. It was a pattern, a way of life that I'd gotten used to without even realizing it. You learn to walk on eggshells. You learn to read moods. You learn to make yourself smaller, quieter, less threatening, hoping that maybe this time he won't explode.

By the help of the Lord, I overcame that situation. It didn't happen overnight. It was slow, bit by bit, day by day. But I began to live a normal life again. I learned to walk. I learned to do things for myself. And I became the mother and father for my two boys.

I had to be both. They needed me to be both. After everything they'd witnessed, all that violence and chaos, I had to show them we could survive. That we could be all right. So I did what I had to do. I raised them by myself, worked hard, made sure they had what they needed.

I would tell them, "I'm not trying to pick your friends, but you shouldn't get involved with that person." And they'd tell me that's their friend and there ain't nothing wrong with him. They didn't want to hear what I had to say, even when I was trying to protect them.

Whenever I learned that they did something wrong, I would take them back to wherever they did it and made them apologize and give back whatever they'd taken. I didn't believe in taking anything from anybody, and I wanted to instill that in them. I wanted them to grow up with integrity, to know right from wrong, to be better than the life I'd lived.

My oldest son, Postosis, he went into the army when he got older. I was very happy that he decided to do something with his life. What better thing to do than serve our country? I thought maybe this was his chance, his way out, his path to something good.

But the happiness didn't last long. When he came home on furlough, his so-called friends got with him and got him interested in other things. Drugs and drinking. One of his friends, they robbed a store together and landed in prison. My son, the one who'd saved my life by running next door that terrible night, was now behind bars.

He pretty much lived with regret. But he wasn't home long before he robbed a store by himself and went back to prison. This boy had been so smart growing up. He played football and was great at it until his growth bone was broken in two. After that, he couldn't play anymore. But he was born with great gifts from God. He was smart in school, ambidextrous, could draw anything. He made jewelry. He had so much potential.

Later in life, he met a nice country girl and they got married. They didn't have any children together, but she had one child. And the same thing that happened with me happened with him. Her parents thought he wasn't good enough for her. But they stayed married anyway, and he passed away several years later with stomach cancer.

My baby boy, Johnny, we called him Mister because he was so smart. He met a neighborhood girl from a little town outside of Austin.

She just liked him for whatever he could do for her, but she got pregnant.

Then he got in trouble. My nephew came by and asked him if he'd go with him to pick up a check from the job. But my nephew told a lie. He went to the place where he worked and robbed it. My son was with him, and my nephew wouldn't tell them that my son didn't have nothing to do with it. He just let it go down like my son knew all about it.

I got him out. I had a lawyer and got him out on shock probation. He went to college and was working and doing good. Then his cousin came by one day, and they went down by the park. They wound up over at the store not far from the park, and the cousin took twenty dollars from a guy.

I didn't learn about it until later. One morning, his brother came by and asked me, "Was Johnny here?" I said yes, he's in there asleep. The brother said the police wanted to come down, just wanted to talk to him, and it wouldn't take long. He'd come back.

But he told a lie. His brother Kevin had signed a statement saying Johnny was the one who took the twenty dollars. Johnny was seventeen years old, and he didn't ever come back to the house. He was sent to prison for ten years. Then when he got in prison, he got into a little trouble and they tacked fourteen years onto that. He stayed twenty-four years flat in the penitentiary.

In the meantime, several different times, he wanted a Bible. I went and bought a Bible and sent it to him because he felt like he had a calling. But then I don't know what happened with that.

One day, he went down to get a haircut. Two guys from a gang strangled him and it made him have massive brain damage.

15

I was called one August morning, right about nine o'clock. It was a chaplain from the penitentiary telling me that Johnny was just hanging on. If I wanted to get to see him and talk to him, I needed to come out there. He said Johnny was in Beaumont.

I had just got out of the hospital myself. I had been in the hospital three months. I had let my nephew borrow my Jeep because I couldn't drive. So I had my nephew bring me my Jeep, and I told some other members of the family. I think mama went with me. I think my daughter-in-law went with me down to Beaumont to see Johnny.

When they let me in the room to see him, they had him all shackled down. His ankles was shackled. His hands was shackled around in his back. I went ballistic. I just had a fit. I said, "Why y'all have him like this? He's in a coma. He don't even know he's in the world." And I had them take those things off of him.

Then I went close up to Johnny and I said, "This is mama, Johnny. Johnny, please don't leave me. Don't leave me, Johnny. We ain't been together like nothing. Johnny, don't leave. Father God, don't let Johnny leave. Father God, please let Johnny stay here with me."

God heard my prayer and blessed Johnny to make it. He came out of that coma. He left Beaumont and went to the hospital in Galveston. From Galveston, he went to MD Anderson Hospital in Houston. Then from there, they sent him back to the penitentiary, but not to the same unit. He went to another unit.

I continued to try to get him out. I continued and continued, and with the help of the Lord, I did get him out. He came out of the penitentiary on December 18, 2006.

I went in the back of the penitentiary, and mama rode with me. I got him and we stopped on the way home and got something to eat. It was a hallelujah day that my child was out of penitentiary after being gone all those years. I just felt great that I had my son home with me.

I had got a nice home so he could have his own room. We had a brand new car. The good Lord blessed Mister and I to be together for five years. I am thankful for that. God blessed us five years together because we hadn't been together since he was seventeen years old. I mean, I would go to the penitentiary and visit him, but you know what I mean. Real contact, being together.

When he came home, they had a parole officer come by, check on him and check his urine. I let her do it about three times. Then I said, "Wait a minute. I'm not having this. It don't make no sense what you're doing. I'm his mother and I'm going to take good care of him. He don't drink and he doesn't do no drugs. I have never allowed nothing like that. And he don't even have a mind or heart to even do that kind of stuff. He's on medication, heavy medication. So what good is it going to do to check his pee when he's taking medication?"

I raised so much stink about it that one of the main officers came out and saw I was taking really good care of my child. They said it doesn't need nobody coming out anymore. So they stopped it. Didn't nobody come out here no more.

Johnny was just like a baby all over again. Using the bathroom on himself and everything. I didn't need no interference in that. God took care of it. It wasn't me. It was God intervening into my well-being and seeing it wasn't necessary. The good Lord blessed us to not be bothered with that.

This was my life as a single mother. Trying to do right by my boys, trying to keep them safe, trying to give them a chance. But life had other plans. The streets pulled them in. Bad influences pulled them in.

And no matter how hard I tried, no matter how strict I was, I couldn't protect them from everything.

That's the aftermath of domestic violence. It's not just the scars on my body from those twenty-seven stab wounds. It's the years of raising children alone, of trying to be both mother and father, of watching them struggle and knowing you can't fix everything. It's the fear that never quite goes away, the way you jump at sudden sounds, the way you check the locks before bed.

But it's also learning that you're stronger than you ever knew. It's discovering that God can heal what seems unhealable. It's finding out that love doesn't give up, even when everything else does.

I survived that night when Big Johnny tried to kill me. But surviving is more than just staying alive. It's learning to live again. And with God's help, that's exactly what I did.

CHAPTER 5

RAISING SONS THROUGH HARDSHIP

When my son Johnny came home after all those years, I felt like my prayers had finally been answered. I went to the back of the penitentiary myself to bring him out, and when he stepped through those gates, it was like God gave me my child back. We stopped to get something to eat on the way home, laughing a little, crying a little, just happy to be together again after so long. I thanked the Lord for blessing me to see that day.

At home, I tried to make things as comfortable as I could for him. I had gotten a nice house so he could have his own room and space to rest. He wasn't the same as before; the years had taken a toll on him, and he needed help with the simple things. But I was just thankful he was alive and back with me. The good Lord had spared his life, and I knew it was my job to take care of him. I didn't mind. I'd been a mother all my life, and I loved him with everything I had.

A parole officer came by at first to check on him, but I didn't see no reason for it. He didn't drink, didn't do drugs, and I made sure he stayed on his medication. I told them straight that I was his mother and I would take good care of him myself. They finally saw that I meant it and stopped coming around. That was God's doing, not mine. He knew I didn't need no extra worry.

The Lord blessed Mister and me to share five good years together after his return. We hadn't had that kind of time since he was seventeen years old, and I cherished every day of it. It wasn't always easy, but I never once forgot how far God had brought us.

Not long after, my mama told me she wanted us to buy a house together. She said we could live under one roof and help each other out. I thought it was a blessing, so we went ahead and did it. But after a few months, she told me one morning she was moving out. I couldn't believe it. She said she didn't want to spend her money helping pay for the house. I tried to talk her out of it, told her I couldn't manage it alone, but she had already made up her mind. By that afternoon, she was gone.

I sat there that night and prayed, asking God to help me forgive her. I told Him I didn't understand why she'd leave me like that after all we'd been through, but I knew I had to let it go. I couldn't carry anger in my heart. I asked the Lord for peace, and He gave it to me.

After she moved out, I did what I could to keep the house. I sold a few things and cut corners, but it wasn't enough. In time, I lost it to foreclosure. It hurt, but I reminded myself that God always makes a way, even when it feels like everything is falling apart. And He did. Somehow, He kept me and my son covered through it all.

Even after what happened, I never stopped loving my mama. Every month, I went to see about her, took her food, paid her bills when she needed help, and made sure she was all right. We'd sit and talk, just like before. She would say, "That sounds good, Carol. I sure could eat some of that," and I'd bring her a plate. That was my way of forgiving her without saying a word.

Those years taught me what real strength is. It's not in how much you can carry, but how much you can still love after being hurt. I had been through loss, violence, and heartbreak, but the hardest part was learning to keep my faith steady when everything around me kept changing.

Raising my sons through hardship wasn't just about surviving. It was about holding on to love, even when life didn't make sense. And through it all, I never stopped trusting the One who brought me this far.

Because I know for certain without God, I wouldn't have made it.

CHAPTER 6

FAMILY TENSIONS AND BETRAYALS

It's a painful thing when the people you love become the ones who hurt you the most. I used to think that family was supposed to be your safe place, but I learned that sometimes, family can become the storm itself. I had already survived so much violence, loss, sickness, and heartbreak, but nothing cut as deep as the betrayal that came from my own blood.

After all I had done to help my family, I never thought they would turn against me. I had given when I didn't have much to give, prayed for them when they were in trouble, and stood by them in times of need. But jealousy has a way of turning love into bitterness. My baby sister's daughters, the ones I helped raise, started acting strange toward me. They whispered behind my back, spread lies, and tried to make others turn away from me. It took me a while to see what was happening because I always tried to see the good in people, especially family.

There were moments when their actions went beyond words. Strange things started happening around me. I began feeling sick for no reason, hearing things that didn't make sense. One day, I felt something in my head, a spot that throbbed with pain that wouldn't go away. I prayed over it, asking the Lord to show me what was going on. The pain got worse, so I finally went to the hospital Seton Hospital. When the doctors examined me, they found something buried in my scalp, something that shouldn't have been there. They removed it, and

I thanked God right there for protecting me. I don't know how it got there, but I knew in my heart that it was no ordinary sickness. I believed someone had meant me harm, but God didn't let it work.

It hurt me deeply to think my own family could wish bad on me. I had always loved them and helped them every way I could. But the more I prayed, the more God revealed that some people around me carried jealousy instead of love. I didn't fight back. I didn't curse them or wish them harm. I just kept praying and asking God to handle it His way.

One of my nieces called me one day, angry for reasons I still don't understand. Her voice was full of hate, and she told me, "You ain't dead yet?" Those words pierced my heart. I had done nothing but love her. I wanted to hang up, but something inside me told me to stay calm. I told her I would pray for her and that I forgave her. Not long after that call, I got a message that she had passed away suddenly. It broke my heart, but it also reminded me how fragile life is. I didn't rejoice in her death; I mourned it. But I also knew God had shown me that He protects His children, even when others wish them harm.

The years that followed brought more loss and confusion. Some of my family members fell into dark paths one was poisoned, another was murdered, and another died in an accident. I don't take joy in any of that. I just see how life has a way of revealing truth over time. What people meant for harm, God turned into proof of His mercy. I am still here because He chose to keep me here.

All I ever wanted was peace in my family. I wanted us to love each other, to forgive, and to lift one another up. But sometimes, no matter how much you try, some hearts refuse to change. I learned to accept that I couldn't fix everyone. I could only pray for them and protect my own peace.

When the tension grew too heavy, I stopped visiting as much. I had to choose my peace over pain. I learned to keep my distance and let God deal with what I couldn't control. I still checked in from time to time, but I no longer let their words or actions steal my joy. I had seen too many miracles in my life to let bitterness take root.

Even in the quiet moments when the memories came back and my heart ached, I reminded myself of one thing: forgiveness is not for them, it's for me. Holding on to anger only makes the wound deeper. So I prayed for each of them by name. I asked God to heal their hearts, to give them peace, and to help me keep mine.

Family betrayal taught me that love and trust don't always come from blood. Sometimes, the people God places in your life later become your real family the ones who pray for you, care for you, and lift you up when you're weak. I thank God for the few who stood by me, even when others turned away.

Looking back now, I can see how every trial prepared me for the next. The betrayals broke something inside me, but they also made me stronger. I learned to depend on God more than ever before. He showed me that no weapon formed against me would prosper. I learned that I didn't need to fight every battle myself. I just needed to keep my heart pure and let Him handle the rest.

Family can bless you or break you. Mine did both. But through it all, I kept my faith. I refused to let hate win. I survived because I chose prayer over anger and peace over revenge. And even though those betrayals left scars, they also proved that the same God who saved me before was still watching over me.

As I moved forward, I carried no grudges. I carried wisdom. I knew who I was in God and what He had brought me through. Every hurt, every loss, every cruel word they all became part of my testimony. The devil tried to destroy me through the people closest to me, but God turned it all into strength.

No matter how many storms my family brought into my life, my faith stood firm. Because when everyone else turned their back on me, the Lord never did. And that truth is what keeps me standing to this day.

Chapter 7

Health Struggles and Miracles

One Sunday evening, out of nowhere, I was hit with the worst pain I had ever felt in my head. It came sudden, like someone had struck me, and it would not let up. I took every kind of pain pill I had in the house Tylenol, aspirin, you name it but nothing worked. I told my son Aavion, "Lord, this pain is something else. It just came right here in my head." I lay down hoping it would pass, but it only got worse.

For two days I tried everything I could to get relief, but by Tuesday I couldn't take it anymore. The pain was so severe I could barely think straight. So I went to the hospital. They ran every kind of test they could think of blood work, scans, everything but still couldn't find a thing. Around two or three o'clock that afternoon a neurologist came in and told me, "Miss Waldon, I'm going to admit you to the hospital."

He said they were going to transfer me to Austin, to Seton Hospital on 38th Street. I agreed because I was desperate for help. When I got there, they gave me a private room and started testing me all over again. They ran brain scans, CAT scans, and all sorts of examinations, but the pain stayed just as strong. No shot or pill could ease it. I prayed the whole time, asking God to touch me and take the pain away.

By Friday I was still in pain when a dermatologist came into my room with his assistant. He introduced himself and said, "I just want to take a look at your head, Miss Waldon." I told him, "Go ahead, doctor. Help yourself, because I can't take this pain anymore."

He looked closely at the top of my head and said he wanted to try something. I told him he could do whatever he needed to do. He took a small instrument from his pocket and gently opened a spot on my scalp. Then, using what looked like tweezers, he pulled out a tiny piece of something from under my skin. The moment he did that, the pain disappeared.

I sat there in shock. I said, "Doctor, let me see it." He showed it to me it looked like a small piece of gristle or bone. I said, "Lord, have mercy." The doctor told me it was something very rare. He said it was unusual to ever see something like that happen. I told him I wanted to keep it, but he said he needed to take it with him for testing. I didn't argue. I was just thankful the pain was gone.

They made me stay another night for observation, just to make sure nothing else happened. But I knew I was already healed. I told the Lord right there in that hospital room, "Thank You, Jesus. You touched me. You stopped the pain when nothing else could."

Later, when I thought about it, I realized this wasn't just sickness it was an attack. Someone had meant harm for me. They wanted my mind to be gone, my body weak, and my spirit broken. But God didn't allow it. He blocked whatever plan was meant against me. What they tried to use to destroy me, God turned into a testimony.

Even the doctors couldn't explain what they found. The dermatologist said it was rare, almost unheard of. But I knew what it was: a miracle. God had shown me again that He was watching over me. He wouldn't let evil win.

As I left the hospital, I thought about everything I had survived violence, heartbreak, betrayal, and now this. Every time someone tried to bring me down, God lifted me higher. Every time pain tried to take me out, He gave me peace instead. I walked out of that hospital praising His name. I knew then that no matter what comes, my life is in His hands. And when I think back on that night the pain, the fear, the healing I know one thing for sure: the Lord was right there with me, and that was the greatest miracle of all.

After I came home, there was one woman someone I'd once helped who showed me how deep jealousy can run. She called and said, "You're not dead yet?" I didn't get angry. I just told her, "No, God hasn't called me yet," and left it at that. A week later she called again, saying she wanted to stay with me "so when you die, I can make sure you're put away nice." I said, "No, ma'am. I can't have drama in my house. If I get sick, it'll be because God allows it, not because of anyone bringing trouble." That was on a Friday. By the next Friday, she was gone.

I didn't rejoice over that. I simply understood God was fighting my battles. Some people had even gone to fortune tellers, paying money to find ways to harm me. I heard later those same fortune tellers told them, "Leave her alone," but they wouldn't listen. What they meant for evil, God turned into proof of His power.

I never let them know that I knew. I didn't argue, threaten, or act hateful. I gave it all to God and kept living my life. I thanked Him for showing me what was done behind my back, but I didn't have to handle it myself. The Lord handled it better than I ever could.

That's when I learned for sure: when you give something to God, you don't take it back. He knows how to set things right in His own time and He surely did.

That hospital stay taught me that miracles still happen. God didn't just heal my body; He opened my eyes. From that day forward, I promised I'd never doubt His power again. I walked out of Seton Hospital lighter, stronger, and more certain than ever that my life is in His hands.

CHAPTER 8

FINDING PEACE AND NEW BEGINNINGS

There came a time when I finally stopped fighting the past. For so many years, my life had been one battle after another people hurting me, sickness taking my strength, and heartache trying to break my spirit. I spent years asking God why certain things had to happen. But somewhere along the way, my prayers changed. I stopped asking why and started saying thank You.

I thanked Him for the strength that got me through it all, for every lesson hidden in my pain, and for the peace that slowly took the place of fear. I realized that peace doesn't come all at once. It comes little by little, like light breaking through after a long night. And when it finally came, I felt it deep in my heart.

These days, I don't let the past weigh me down anymore. I still remember it, but it doesn't hurt like it used to. I can talk about what happened and not feel bitterness. I can look at the scars on my body and see survival instead of suffering. Every mark, every memory, every tear they all remind me of how far God has carried me.

The same people who once tried to bring me down don't hold any power over me now. I pray for them. I ask God to give them peace too. I know forgiveness isn't about letting someone off the hook it's about freeing yourself from the pain they left behind. When I learned that, I started living again.

After all the storms I've been through, I find joy in the simplest things. I wake up in the morning and thank God just for another day.

I sit by the window and watch the sunrise, knowing I almost didn't live to see it. I talk with my nephew and feel hope for the future. I don't need much just peace in my heart and the presence of God by my side. That's more than enough.

I've learned that healing isn't just about your body getting better. It's about your heart finding rest. My peace didn't come from doctors, money, or people it came from faith. Faith taught me that God can use pain to build purpose. He can take what was meant for harm and turn it into something good.

There was a time I used to cry myself to sleep wondering if life would ever get better. Now, I go to sleep thanking God that it already has. I'm not the same woman I used to be. I've grown stronger, wiser, and softer all at the same time. I've learned that peace doesn't mean life is perfect it means I've made peace with imperfection.

Sometimes people ask me how I keep smiling after everything I've lived through. I tell them it's simple: I've seen what God can do. He kept me alive when death was at my door. He healed my mind when others wanted it gone. He brought light into places where there was nothing but darkness. How could I not smile after that?

I used to think survival was the goal, but now I see that peace is the real blessing. Surviving makes you stronger, but peace makes you whole. I don't carry anger anymore. I don't worry about what I lost. Instead, I thank God for what I still have my mind, my spirit, and a story worth telling.

Every day feels like a new beginning. I take time to enjoy the small moments the sound of birds in the morning, the laughter of family, the quiet stillness of prayer. I've learned that joy doesn't have to be loud. Sometimes it's just sitting still and knowing you're loved by God.

When I look back over my life now, I don't see a trail of pain. I see a trail of miracles. I see proof that no matter how many times you fall, faith can lift you again. I see how God turned every wound into wisdom.

I may not have everything I once dreamed of, but I have peace and that's something I never thought I'd find. I've forgiven those who hurt me, I've let go of the pain, and I've given all the glory to God. My life is no longer about what I've lost, but about what I've gained: faith, peace, and a heart that still believes in love.

The woman I am now is not the same woman who started this journey. I walk slower, I speak softer, and I love deeper. I live each day knowing that every breath is a gift.

If there's one thing my story proves, it's that peace is possible after pain. You can be broken and still be blessed. You can lose everything and still find yourself. And when you finally do, you'll understand what I do now peace isn't found in the absence of storms, but in trusting the One who calms them.

That's my new beginning. Not the end of my story, but the part where I finally rest in God's peace and let His love define who I am.

CHAPTER 9

THE BLESSING OF STILLNESS

After everything I had been through, the house finally grew quiet. The noise that once filled my days arguments, crying, worry, and pain was gone. At first, the silence felt strange. I wasn't used to peace. I had lived so long in chaos that when life slowed down, I didn't know what to do with the stillness. But in that quiet, I began to feel something new. I began to feel God's presence in a deeper way than ever before.

Each morning, I would wake up and thank Him for letting me see another day. It wasn't just words anymore, it was gratitude that came from the bottom of my heart. I didn't rush like I used to. I'd sit for a moment, listen to the birds, and breathe in the peace that surrounded me. That peace was hard-earned. I had fought through storms to reach it.

There was a time when I didn't think I'd make it to this season. The pain I carried emotional and physical had taken so much from me. But now, I was learning that peace isn't the absence of problems; it's the calm that God places in your heart while the world still spins around you.

Some days I'd sit in my chair and just talk to the Lord. I didn't need to ask for much anymore. My prayers turned into conversations simple thank-yous, small praises. I realized that peace isn't something you chase. It's something that grows inside you when you stop fighting against what's already been written.

The hurt, the betrayal, the sickness they no longer had power over me. I could remember it all without feeling bitterness. That's when I knew I was healing for real. My heart was no longer heavy. I had learned to let things go. People who once tried to hurt me no longer lived in my mind rent-free. I gave them all to God.

I didn't have everything I once dreamed of, but I had peace and that was more valuable than anything else. I had food on my table, a roof over my head, and the comfort of knowing I wasn't alone. God had been my provider, my healer, my protector. And now, in the stillness of my life, I could see His hand in everything.

There were moments when I would reflect on how far I'd come. The woman I used to be the one who worried, cried, and tried to fix everything herself had been replaced by a woman who trusted God with it all. I didn't carry those burdens anymore. I learned that when you truly give something to God, you stop reaching for it again.

Peace taught me to appreciate the little things I once overlooked. The sunlight coming through my window, a quiet meal, a good night's sleep those were gifts I used to take for granted. Now, they felt holy.

Sometimes I'd walk outside and feel the wind on my face and just whisper, "Thank You, Lord." That's all I needed to say. I didn't need long prayers or big words. Just gratitude.

I think God brings us to stillness for a reason. We spend so much time running from pain that we forget healing often happens when we finally stop moving. In my stillness, He restored my spirit. He reminded me that even though I had walked through dark valleys, I was never walking alone.

People sometimes ask how I can be so calm after everything that happened. I tell them it's because I've seen what God can do. When you've been through fire and survived, you stop fearing the smoke. When you've been broken and God puts you back together, you learn to trust His hands.

I used to pray for deliverance; now I pray for peace. And He's given it to me. Not the kind of peace that depends on everything going right, but the kind that stays even when life still has its ups and downs.

The stillness I live in now isn't empty. It's full full of gratitude, full of presence, full of God. I've learned to enjoy being alive without waiting for the next storm to come. Every day feels like a quiet blessing.

Looking back, I understand that the silence I once feared was the very thing that saved me. It gave me space to hear God's voice again. It gave me rest. And in that rest, I found renewal.

I don't know what tomorrow holds, but I'm not afraid of it anymore. The same God who brought me through every battle will meet me there, too. I'm at peace with my story, my past, and my present. That peace is my reward for everything I've endured.

This is what I call the blessing of stillness, where you stop running from what was and start living in what is. It's where you finally understand that peace doesn't just happen. It's something you let God place in your heart, one quiet day at a time.

CHAPTER 10

A LIFE OF TESTIMONY

I've come to see my whole life as a testimony. Every trial, every tear, every night I thought would never end it was all leading me here. For a long time, I didn't understand why I had to go through so much pain. But now I know it was so I could tell somebody else that God is real.

There was a time when I was too shy to speak about what He had done for me. I thought people wouldn't believe it, or they would judge me for the things I had lived through. But I don't feel that way anymore. When you've seen the Lord heal your body and protect your mind, you stop worrying about what others think. I speak because I've seen His power.

Sometimes people come to me with stories of their own broken homes, sickness, betrayal, loss and I listen. I tell them I understand. I tell them how God carried me when I couldn't carry myself. I don't preach; I just share. My story is proof that faith still works.

I never planned to be anyone's example. I'm just a woman who's been through a lot and found peace on the other side. But if my story can give someone else hope, then that's what I'll do. When I talk about how I almost lost my mind, how the pain in my head nearly took me out, and how the Lord stepped in, people see the truth of it. They see that no medicine or money could have done that. Only God.

These days, I don't keep my testimony to myself. At church, I stand up and thank God for His goodness. I tell them how He saved me from the hands of the enemy and gave me back my life. Sometimes my voice shakes, but I speak anyway. I'm not ashamed of what I've been through. My past is no longer a burden it's a bridge that connects me to others who are hurting.

I've learned that you don't need a pulpit to share the gospel. You can testify in your living room, at the grocery store, or sitting on your front porch. Wherever someone needs encouragement, that's your ministry. I never went looking for it, but the Lord made my life one.

Every time I tell my story, I feel that same peace rise up in me again. It reminds me that I didn't come this far alone. I think of all the times I could have given up, and how God wouldn't let me. He turned every broken piece into part of a testimony I can carry proudly.

People sometimes ask, "Don't you get tired of talking about what happened?" I tell them no. Because every time I speak it, I remember that I'm still here. I remember that the devil tried, but he failed. I remember that what was meant for evil turned into something good. That's worth telling as long as I live.

Even at home, when it's quiet, I'll talk to the Lord and thank Him for using me. I know my life hasn't been easy, but it's been meaningful. Every challenge became a chapter, and every victory became a verse in my song of praise.

If someone had told me years ago that my pain would help others heal, I wouldn't have believed them. But now I see that's exactly what God does, He turns misery into ministry. He takes the things that almost destroyed you and makes them the reason someone else keeps going.

I may never write a sermon or stand behind a pulpit, but I live one every day. When I pray for a friend, when I tell my story without shame, that's my testimony in action.

I'm grateful that God didn't let my story end in pain. He turned it into a purpose. He gave me a reason to speak, a reason to live, and a reason to praise. My life is proof that you can come through fire and still shine.

So I keep telling it how I was hurt but healed, betrayed but blessed, broken but restored. Because every word gives God glory, and as long as I have breath, I'll keep testifying.

That's my calling now, not to relive the past, but to remind others that God still performs miracles, that faith still changes lives, and that peace is possible for anyone who believes.

This is my life of testimony born out of pain, built on grace, and carried by faith.

CHAPTER 11

LEGACY AND LOVE

Family has always been at the center of my life. I have loved every one of them the good, the troubled, the ones who helped me, and even the ones who turned against me. No matter what happened, my heart never let go. God gave me that kind of heart, one that remembers love more than pain.

I know there are folks out there going through the same kinds of trials I faced. I tell them, "Hang in there with God. Give it all to Him and be still. Don't pick it back up once you've laid it down. He'll work it out." I've seen Him do it over and over again in my own family.

One of my nieces went her own way for a while. She ended up with one of her cousins, and together they had two boys. Thank God those boys came into the world healthy and strong. I pray they grow up knowing that God's mercy is bigger than any mistake. I still love their mother and wish her peace. Love doesn't stop just because people stumble.

Through the years, I've lost so many of my brothers and sisters. Each one left a mark on my heart.

My sister Faye suffered terribly before she passed from cancer. My brother Clarence everybody called him Ski was shot in the back of the head and laid out like he was sleeping. My brother Steve, whose real name was Cleveland, was shot in the heart with a .38 revolver. One of my little sisters was run over out on the hill where we grew up and thrown beside the highway.

And then there was my brother Choc. His story still hurts to tell.

For a time he lived wild. There was a woman who spoiled him bought him name-brand clothes and gold rings with his initials, even sent him on planes from Austin to Dallas to watch the Cowboys. But both of them were using drugs, and my brother fell deeper than she did. He started on heroin until he burned the vein in his ankle and had to use the ones in his foot. It was destroying him.

The woman tried to quiet folks by giving me her old clothes so I wouldn't talk about her being with my brother, but that wasn't going to shut me up forever. She had a brother playing for the Dallas Cowboys and didn't want her secret out. When things got too hot, she ran back to Dallas and left my brother tangled in debt and addiction.

My cousin his cousin too, my mama's sister's boy had a job, nice car, good life. But he went and talked my brother into robbing a store. That was the end of my brother's freedom. He got more than a hundred years in the penitentiary.

For a while, they still allowed furloughs. Every few years, he'd come home for a weekend, and I'd go pick him up myself, drive all the way to Lovelady, where the Eastham Unit sits, or sometimes to the McClellan Unit. I picked him up four different times. We'd eat good meals, laugh a little, and then I'd drive him back on Sunday. He always called me Shine. He said once, "Shine, they told me if I come back to this place again, I won't make it out alive." I told him, "Then don't go back. Talk to God and start over. He can give you a better life." But the world is hard on men with records. He couldn't find work, and before long he was back inside.

He always worked in the kitchen, thought he could out-cook the cooks. He kept a big jar of lemonade or Kool-Aid with him because it got so hot back there. Two times before he'd been poisoned and made deathly sick. The third time they put more in his drink, enough to kill him. The chaplain called me late one Friday night almost midnight to say my brother was gone. I was getting my clothes ready to visit him that next day. I remember just standing there, too numb to cry. I loved him unconditionally, the way God loves us.

I told them to send him to Cook-Walden Funeral Home on Lamar. I'd promised him that if anything ever happened, I'd see he was put away nice. I had him insured, and I liked Cook-Walden because you could do everything there buy the suit, the vault, the headstone.

But his body kept swelling, and they didn't have a suit to fit him. A friend of mine gave me one of his own suits same color, same style as the one Cook-Walden was going to use. They charged me for it anyway. I wanted an upright headstone, not one that lay flat, but they did what they wanted, maybe because of what he'd been accused of. I even ordered a vault and never knew if they put it in the ground. I've thought about getting a court order to find out, but it's been years now.

I heard later that the officer who poisoned him didn't live much longer himself. It never made the news, but word got around that he was killed not long after. It was all heartbreaking. My brother had already suffered enough. I had to hurry to bury him because of the swelling, and it still haunts me sometimes.

Even after all of that, I never stopped loving him. When people ask how I can talk about these things without bitterness, I tell them it's because love doesn't die when people do it just changes shape. I pray for every one of my brothers and sisters. I talk to God about them often, thanking Him for the time we had and the strength to keep loving through it all.

41

When I look at the next generations my nieces, and nephews I want them to know where they come from and to hold their heads high. Our story isn't perfect, but it's real. Every trial taught us something about faith, forgiveness, and endurance.

To the ones still living, I keep saying: *God hasn't forgotten you.* No matter what you've done, His mercy can reach you where you are. Prayer changes things, even when people don't.

My family's story is more than tragedy; it's testimony. Out of all that pain came a strength only God could give. We've buried too many, but the love remains. I carry it with me every day, and I honor them by living in peace.

When the house is quiet, I sometimes hear their laughter again the way we used to talk long after the sun went down. Those memories comfort me. They remind me that family is more than blood; it's the spirit that ties us together through everything.

I may be one of the last ones still standing, but I'm standing with gratitude. God let me live long enough to tell this story not to bring sorrow, but to show that love endures even when the world falls apart. That's my legacy. Not the pain, not the losses, but the love that kept us all connected through it all.

EPILOGUE

THE LORD CARRIED ME

Before you judge my life, my past, my character, walk in my shoes. Walk the path I've traveled. Live my sorrow, my doubts, my fear, my pain, and my laughter. Remember, everyone has a story. When you live my life, then you can judge me.

As I sit and look back over my life, all I can say is that God has been good to me. I've been through the fire, through pain I wouldn't wish on anybody, but I'm still here. And it's not because I was strong it's because the Lord carried me.

There were times I didn't know if I would make it. There were days when my body hurt and my heart hurt even worse. But every time I thought I couldn't take another step, God lifted me up and kept me moving forward. I know now that it wasn't my strength that brought me this far; it was His mercy.

I thank Him every morning I wake up. I thank Him for peace, for health, for the chance to see another sunrise. When I was young, I used to rush through life, always fighting to survive. Now I take my time. I breathe. I listen. I notice things I once overlooked the sound of the birds, the way the light falls through the window, the quiet comfort of prayer. These are blessings too.

I don't have everything I ever wanted, but I have everything I need. I have love in my heart, forgiveness in my spirit, and peace in my home. That's more than I could ask for. The same God who brought me through sickness, betrayal, and loss gave me something greater than all of that contentment.

Sometimes I think about all the people who are gone now, all the family I've loved and buried. And I realize that even though they're no longer here, the love we shared still lives in me. That love keeps me company when the house is quiet. It reminds me that I was never truly alone.

When I talk to God now, I don't ask Him for much. I just thank Him for keeping His promises. He told me He would never leave me, and He never did. Even when I was broken, He was there holding the pieces. Even when people turned their backs on me, He turned my pain into purpose.

If there's one thing I've learned in this life, it's that faith will take you further than fear ever could. I used to worry about tomorrow, but now I know who holds tomorrow. The same God who carried me then will carry me wherever I go next.

So when people ask how I survived everything I've been through, I tell them simply: I didn't do it alone. The Lord carried me. He carried me through sickness, through sorrow, through betrayal, and through loss. He carried me when I was too weak to walk, when I was too tired to pray, and when I didn't think I could go on.

And now, as I live out these quiet days, I carry Him in my heart. I carry His peace, His strength, and His love everywhere I go. My story isn't one of defeat, it's a testimony of faith. God took what was meant to destroy me and turned it into something beautiful.

I don't know what tomorrow holds, but I'm not afraid of it anymore. I've seen what He can do. I've felt His healing hands and His comfort in my darkest nights. Whatever comes next, I know I'll be alright.

Because after everything that's happened after every loss, every prayer, every miracle I know one thing for sure.

The Lord carried me, and He still does.

Lord, you kept me. You never left me. It's easy for me to explain. God's grace. It was God's grace that made that I made it this far. He's amazing grace. I sit back and look over the years. Lord, I thank you.